CALL OF THE STORM

LUKE ADITSAN

BALBOA.
PRESS

A DIVISION OF HAY HOUSE

Balboa Press books may be ordered through booksellers or by contacting:

Balboa Press
A Division of Hay House
1663 Liberty Drive
Bloomington, IN 47403
www.balboapress.com
1-(877) 407-4847

Because of the dynamic nature of the Internet, any web addresses or links contained in this book may have changed since publication and may no longer be valid. The views expressed in this work are solely those of the author and do not necessarily reflect the views of the publisher, and the publisher hereby disclaims any responsibility for them.

The author of this book does not dispense medical advice or prescribe the use of any technique as a form of treatment for physical, emotional, or medical problems without the advice of a physician, either directly or indirectly. The intent of the author is only to offer information of a general nature to help you in your quest for emotional and spiritual well-being. In the event you use any of the information in this book for yourself, which is your constitutional right, the author and the publisher assume no responsibility for your actions.

Any people depicted in stock imagery provided by Thinkstock are models, and such images are being used for illustrative purposes only.

Certain stock imagery © Thinkstock.

ISBN: 978-1-4525-6537-8 (sc)
ISBN: 978-1-4525-6538-5 (e)

Library of Congress Control Number: 2012923400

Printed in the United States of America

Balboa Press rev. date: 12/18/2012

minnow

darting within a puny puddle
oh mighty minnow lost at sea
with memories
of yonder pond
pulled apart by the heat of the day.

why, silvery one,
did you linger
at the edge of your universe
where shallow temptations
whisper?

fear of the deep
I suppose
where large-jawed demons
lurk
beyond waving fronds.

but now alone
in a cringing pocket
of fiery water
stranded
as an abandoned child.

are bitty minnows heard
when they cry to the skies
hoping
fearing
as they lap with pulsing gills?

heavy clouds
array for battle
steaming across the heavens
as if the tiniest prayer
summoned.

across the earth
rainfall spatters here and there
like the dancing shadow
of a butterfly
free.

rivulets link
as worlds grow
and the cool oceans full of demons
seem not so
ominous.

The Forest Man

The hugeness of land surrounded by seas,
a drafty kingdom amidst oceans of trees,
rushing citizens replete with thought,
gabs and gibits rigorously wrought,

from bare spot thatches some doing flows,
wrangling plants from neat little rows,
cascading mews of a distant fiddle,
near fortress throne in the middle in the middle,

castle dotted with droves of doors,
mazy paths with flattened stone floors,
patterned cloth shimmies in the breeze,
a crowning banner amidst oceans of trees,

his liege now listens with chin in hand,
a crushing job to govern this land,
serious was he even now with blues,
his sole vocation, himself to amuse,

two geese high up shunning the stink,
of barns and shapers while they tink,
but yet unseen past the cows and the plows,
the uncivil heaven down past the boughs,

half eyed lions lying in the shade,
ducks and swans keeping watch in the glade,
scampering crits slide under a leaf,
a bear a-wading, paws at the reef,

a delicate deer with a flinching flag,
wolves look back when fuzzy pups lag,
this teeming forest lively with life,
this vastful kingdom shows no strife,

from a set vantage peak all would seem well,
but poor prospects hide a visualized hell,
sits blithesome town neath a hanging cloud,
blankets the bustlers neath a mindful shroud,

for once per year awakes a great gust,
unstoppable force dragging mountains of dust,
a vast hand wipes firm across the land,
a display of fury, so stark and so grand,

this disaster strikes at the end of each year,
this final month all would fear,
exact the day, none could bring light,
the cliche be called, a thief in the night,

a bored king would then repeat his norm,
as he sealed himself from this cyclic storm,
the winds would wail and for his trouble,
his castle entirely would be crushed into rubble,

the townsfolk's huts that speckled the ley,
boldly flattened by the close of the day,
homeless all in the kingdom become,
from the terror that thumped it's terrible drum,

all possessions owned inside and out,
batted to oblivion with a mighty clout,
even peeping crops in the ground get razed,
leaving hopeless shells stumbling a-dazed

tender forest life crashed through change,
as the squall the woods would rearrange,
burrows, nests and caves would disappear,
some timberlands tall, now were clear,

wolves, otter, deer, eagles and ducks,
skunks, squirrels, snakes, egrets and chucks,
no calendars had they to help soothsay,
their souls completely were in today,

natural hideouts strewn all a-strew,
what's an enlightened one to do?
no effort, new burrows to seek and find,
and live in the moment, pay storm no mind,

but citizens openly chronology kept,
some when storm's due openly wept,
no sleep to fall though gone to bed,
all in the village would anxiously dread,

storm's aftermath, oh all is lost,
unbearable undoing was the cost,
gathered supplies, gadgets, and gear,
to lose these things was the greatest fear,

some built stronger but all in vain,
others would worry themselves insane,
still more would gather as much as they could,
and deny storm's coming as it always would,

thinkers and reasoners hired by king,
a method to delay this savage sting,
mayhaps a dance would halt the torrent,
or stairs to the heavens to calm the abhorrent,

so time would pass as they checked off the date,
and rebuilt the kingdom with a pensive wait,
life would be perfect, joyous and warm,
if only it weren't for the terrible storm,

dayspring arose across hushed abodes,
a bundle inched slowly o'er misty roads,
farmers roused while the sky made shine,
as a baby crawls, lost to a tree-line,

hours waste, working their wares to tweak,
production's mumbling din, broken by a shriek,
a frantic mother whisks, wearing a blouson,
screaming loud above the babel, "My babies gone!!",

the town unites, all in a row,
through brush and trees, the search went slow,
two tedious days all looked for the child,
finally resigned he was eaten by the wild,

the town took a day for those needing to mourn,
as babe was playing 'neath stalks of corn,
then soon he found a hollow to keep,
with cushions of leaves on which to sleep,

days of tears when needs were not met,
giggling and smiles when needs he would get,
the universe cuddled this lilliputian elf,
granting the lessons he taught himself,

crawling to forage, never fell ill,
if sensing others, held very still,
drank from a stream very near by,
and lie on his back looking up at the sky,

agonized not about repaying a kings loan,
no need to worry bout seeds he had sown,
noone said, go milk morrow's cow,
for all his days, he endured in the now,

but then a day, last month of the year,
destructive wall of wind, destined to shear,
utter rendings, both sticks and rocks,
dwellings demolished less maybe the locks,

buried the valued, some folks did,
fortified places, things they hid,
but to no matter were made these moves,
a storm as this, all hidings removes,

so hushes a time when storms blow over,
much to the relief of the tinker and drover,
the castle in pieces viewed by a hauler,
maybe, he reasoned, the king would think smaller,

the villager's builds to again rebuild,
proving that they were again strong-willed,
as all they owned had been broken and shred,
they secretly harbored the feeling of dread,

amidst the lightning and bursts of thunder,
the forest child's hollow was ripped a-sunder,
the child shortly found a nook to sleep,
and gathered some berries, a safe place to keep,

storm he forgot, no calendar to mark,
only today's songs need he hark,
songs of bright birds greeting the sun,
finding new twigs, having God's fun

that becomes new which loses the old,
that becomes pliable which loses the bold,
knowing of ends paints self full of fear,
knowing of nows brings Spirit so near,

year by year ever time's impact,
storm by storm, the unavoidable fact,
a babe grows up, a divinely timed plan,
dubbed by the puzzled, the Forest Man,

from a tree-line he crept, slowly crept into town,
the astounded gathered from all around,
disheveled, wild looking, and very shy,
yet obvious to all, a gleam to his eye,

thought they his manners a little crude,
the way he fed seemed very rude,
with patience they taught him over time,
to coarsely communicate through sounds and mime,

the townsfolk then asked him bout the storm that was due,
he shrugged and smiled and so silent too,
all is destroyed, to him they'd explain,
a day of great sorrow, misery and pain,

he finally spoke without a doubt,
"I know not what you talk about",
a gentle breeze, all was hushed,
he didn't know about the wind that crushed!!

he spoke again, his face they'd scour,
"Whatever worries you has no power",
a distant robin in the woods was heard,
but from the citizens, not a word,

people's minds spun at his words said coolly,
confusion and uproar, becoming unruly,
the king saw this man being held in odd awe,
time, thought the ruler, to lay down the law,

"For questions." The king said of the arrest,
"To find out who he's trying to best."
He sat Forest Man in a tiny chair,
and glared hard at him to sink in a scare,

the ruler then asked of this small bearded sir,
"Says you the storm never does stir?"
"that no power has this wind we dread?"
"that it is you who are all powerful instead?"

Forest Man then noticed a crow in the sky,
and answered blankly as he watched it fly,
"I know of no storm of which to cower"
"therefore any storm has no power"

beware of a monarch miffed and annoyed,
his kingdom depended on the winds to avoid,
this man he declared, he would not release,
instead he'd be charged with disturbing the peace,

then an example of Forest Man to be,
hung by his arms from a tree,
for all to see in the center of town,
dare not anyone cut him down,

by his majesty's word, Forest Man hung,
all who passed by, his eyes they'd shun,
days passed and his efforts became weak,
as he would glance to the tree-line o'er by the creek,

miracles are the path happenings take,
tis was the month the winds were to awake,
as fact of matter to all's dismay,
this was the unfortunate day,

the great storm lashed, panic raced forth and back,
smashing homes down with a howling whack,
belongings were propelled far thru the air,
landing in oceans in who knows where,

great cries screeched thru town at storm's end,
battered people start looking to fend,
off next year's great and terrible storm,
as they mark their calendars, true to form,

but as of the forest man, the winds blew,
loosening his ties, giving freedom anew,
from these winds he was given new birth,
to him all was given, all of his worth,

he loped thru the tree-line o'er by the creek,
into a depression with stealthy technique,
pulling branches over to form a nest,
getting him home for much needed rest.

A sunny morning, forage for food,
a very happy day, so was his mood,
now is the only day he has ever known,
and neither any calendars does he own,

The townsfolk now busy with work,
some consider the Forest Man a quirk,
some though regard with thoughts so warm,
known as the man who conquered the storm,

lodges, carts, swords and more,
all fall forever to the floor,
a luscious garden abundant to all,
given to us to conquer the squall.

Drumbeats of Heaven

round the crackling
the circle wound
wide eyed young ones
listened
as an oldster stooping
spoke

of approaching clouds
nearing puffs of dark grey blooms
growling
like thousands of horse-hooves
on hollow ground
calling out

danger
like colliding boulders
throwing streaks of spark
as to do harm
as if a loudly earthquake roared
in the skies.

these my children
are not the bodeful warnings
of wind and water
daring to carry away your possessions
breaking false longings
to gather

but rather these bellowing chords
are the drumbeats of heaven
with a message of love
for the tribe
of all life
below.

for without precious water
the rock could not flower
and without precious wind
the trees could not travel
to bear their gifts
of seed

and of the twisting trails of light
making shore on earth
not to burn
nor destroy
like an angry general
determined

but as a gleaming bridge
for the descent of angels
to answer prayers
of we
who have built the fence
of self

and of the wind
a final promise
as it pushes
and in time hushes
that again it will touch the cheek
with grace.

Savannah Son

A land that imaginings ne'er to touch
the make-believe wildlife seem as such
critters that bellow monstrous sounds
or springing delicates with leaps and bounds

skinny runners that chase striped horses
or laughing dogs with bone-breaking forces
tubby bathers with a cavernous yawn
or furry hunters that creep after dawn

raging rivers from mountains high
tree busy jungles that block the sky
lakes so huge they change the weather
brown mud banks that seem as leather

reed filled swamps of oozing mush
savannah that stretches from desert to bush
this of creation, Beauty's supplement
here and there, a human settlement

a Beautiful child to a village born
the name of Blessings given from Love
a mistful sunrise from a mild morn
a Beautiful child to a village born
so smile gentle a mother to adorn
throng of ovations throughout thereof
a Beautiful child to a village born
the name of Blessings given from Love

This living village of savannah and sun
to each a mission all working as one
children romp to try and feel
their mythical plays are near to real

the older of body bunch at the well
impressing witnesses with stories to tell
a group of men bricking a hut
amorous couples behind doors shut

the village healer collects his herbs
all are watchful that he's not disturbed
when outsiders motor the path as a street
everyone joins this stranger to greet

roles evolved as families changed,
romance is free, no loves are arranged
time passes kindly as it sometimes can
as Blessings grows into a young man

A mother teaches her son of prayer
of magical answers to soothe the Heart
for aiding all with guidance and care
a mother teaches her son of prayer
to portion Love's bounty for all to share
a Life of Hope for all to take part
a mother teaches her son of prayer
of magical answers to soothe the Heart

Deep in the jungle secret from light
slinks a general who lives to fight
each child kidnapped is his tool
love of violence is his school

creep upon homesteads with knives and guns
kills while taking daughters and sons
claims from God he was given a sign
this heartless rogue, this roving swine

for him to steal was the norm
the devil wears a uniform
wiping innocence from the eyes
a freedom fighter, his disguise

some say no evil exists in this world
but surely a fiendish flag has unfurled
to scare out signs of compassion mild
to steal away virtue from a very young child

When we pray for midday shade
rain may pour from newborn clouds
Love's answers not custom made
when we pray for midday shade
Heaven's plans are mysteriously laid
the answers can be mighty loud
when we pray for midday shade
rain may pour from newborn clouds

A raid this villain and his young
to steal the young by the end of a gun
of Blessing's village they would look
Blessing's sister, her they took

one could hear them as they boast
they slipped away like a ghost
but Blessings followed out of sight
as the young man trailed although afright

miles through grass and bush they walked,
the uniforms pushed as they laughed and talked
as came the watching sun to set,
Blessings still they hadn't met

finally they empty to a large base camp
a tattered green tent was lit by lamp
there where several grown soldiers be
children all about one could see

Spirit of Love, please hear my plea
guard my sister with your sword
so future moments her I'll see
Spirit of Love, please hear my plea
help her endure this turbulent sea
these rapids of danger let her ford
Spirit of Love, please hear my plea
guard my sister with your sword

Blessings lie blended on the edge
he spotted standing as if on a ledge
the army's leader, big and tall
near the tent watching all

the man was pointing and with a shout
as children all hurried about
yelling orders to those who're fair
it seemed he gave them quite the scare

a booming crack echoed around
as pattering raindrops touched the ground
beads of water off leaves would fall
roaring thunder issued a call

Blessings stood up and approached the king,
his face lit up in a flash of lightning
all looked at him with staggering wonder,
the general grinned, this seemed a blunder

courage bestowed afore a fight
to Love's champion given power
proof of light in the night
courage bestowed afore a fight
a standing flower shows it's might
the hidden strength in summer's shower
courage bestowed afore a fight
to Love's champion given power

Raindrops now stomped like lead
running streams 'cross Blessing's head
as the driving torrent sounded as one
David and Goliath had now begun

"All these children now will leave!"
Blessings shouted while heavens heaved
"Kill him!" laughed the leader loud
but no one moved in this youthful crowd

it had been many a year,
since this leader had this much fear,
he shoved misgivings to the side
and towards Blessings he started to stride

a dripping machete in his hand
to cut down a boy's final stand
he crossed the clearing between the two
and raised his arm, machete too

oh Purity's gate swings swift and wide,
when claiming her property back,
merciless, the angels push harm aside
oh Purity's gate swings swift and wide
place in the Heart the honor to abide,
and prepare a Divine attack,
oh Purity's gate swings swift and wide
when claiming her property back

Poised but a second the madman stood
holding the machete as high as he could
looking down with a booming laugh
like taking to slaughter an innocent calf

a blinding flash but a moment stayed,
lightning's precision striking the blade,
steady groans like a castle door
a giant collapses with thunder's roar

this final glimpse of the general's sight
was a young boy's face lit up by light
now the king, a smoking heap
dead as dead, no soul to keep,

the grown up soldiers gaped in awe
at what their eyes clearly saw
then in fear they turned and ran
from this unknown very young man

afore the innocent, forces would hew
unfalls the child forfended by Faith
unguided reapers are given their due
afore the innocent, forces would hew
Love's storms liberate as on cue
none the blessed will they scathe
afore the innocent, forces would hew
unfalls the child forfended by Faith

A land that imaginings ne'er to touch
the make-believe wildlife seem as such
critters that bellow monstrous sounds
or springing delicates with leaps and bounds

raging rivers from mountains high
tree busy jungles that block the sky
lakes so huge they change the weather
brown mud banks that seem as leather

in this place a village small
a circle of children 'round an old man tall
from the west approached a squall
troubled the children seated all

the old man then told them a story
about a freeing storm of glory
ignored then they, this stormy gale
listening intently to Blessing's tale.

children saved by one of they
who stood by the calling thunder
whose only weapon was to pray
children saved by one of they
thru certain death did he stay
as storms tossed the bad asunder
children saved by one of they
who stood by the calling thunder

Endless Beauty

Sought as I did
with knees to the earth
to sow beauty upon barren land
brought to my aware
by imaginings

hardened ground
layered with slithering sands
I pressed my seeds
of frankincense and myrrh
down

only to skitter to nowhere
with the wind-tossed sand
torturing my plans of beauty
for this ruthless place
suffering

watching my travails
a close-by band of woman led girls
wearing colored hijabs
in silence
amused

at my attempts to sow fineness
on restless land
I lamented
surely the Gods of these lands
had deserted

then stepped forward a child girl
they called Malala
the sweetness of honey
who leaned over to me
shining

she placed a finger
so near to my eye
and held it still as I focused
seeing firstly nought
straining

until at once apparent
a tiny grain of sand
resting on the edge of her finger
like upon a universe of flesh
a tiny star

I watched intense
as the speck seemed to enlarge
till I was entranced by a small round world
covered completely
in garden

a magnificent garden
with fig trees and palms
and meadows of flowers
red, blue, and bright white
flowing

with birds unlike any
soaring limb to limb
with colors so marvelous
this majestic garden oasis
upon a fingertip

a gust broke my stare
as the crumb flew away
and the sand at my knees scrambled
taking my last planted seed
of hoped for fairness

but now my heart knows
millions of worlds
of splendorous beauty
all hereabouts
as each tiny grain surrounding I
a wind sown paradise

Desert Woman

'Such are the laws given by God to our desert city...'

Opening a crack betrayed by a squeak,
a sliver of light slashed cross the floor,
she pressed her sight to the portal to peek,
could anyone hear from near the door?

reassured, she latched it with a clack,
no needless worry about the round pane,
Volunteers had painted the glass black,
block sight of a woman to keep men sane.

'Women must cover every inch of their body...'

she walked a step to her cradled child,
with a loving tilt she beheld her daughter
and began to sing a lullaby mild,
sublime melody that made her eyes water.

softly, so softly, so no man could hear,
this secret song of astounding beauty,
the love of a mother despite the fear,
not to be heard by males was her duty --

'Women can be beat by their husbands at any sign of insubordination...'

"Oh my daughter, you're heart is so pure,
sleep my sweet and kiss the sky,
with my love to hold you sure,
sleep my sweet and don't you cry"

she finished her song at cradle's giggle,
and wished for her a life so free,
the little one then to kick and wiggle,
what kind of test would her coming days be?

'By law a woman must have a male guardian...'

planets whirl and spin as souls change,
relentless time as life it molds,
this woman a wondrous cake she'd arrange,
her precious daughter is nine years old.

a mother's now unspoken fear,
mayhaps some lecher vying a plan
to pluck her daughter from her home here
and marry her to a sixty year man.

'There is no age limit for a female to be married....'

a school for girls, she to start,
to teach of life and worldly things,
to partake of knowledge and make them smart,
to stop the needle of ignorance sting.

she taught her daughter in this space,
defying laws with each guiding breath,
defiantly dodging the Volunteers chase,
defiantly averting a vicious death.

'Girls cannot be educated after age 8...'

one hot day that this desert had made,
the school was crushed with an iron rod,
ranting volunteers conducted their raid,
the long bearded ones in the name of God.

flails and screams punched the peace,
all were gathered and thrown in a bus,
the school's learning now would cease
as in the city was created a fuss.

'By law women are not allowed to work...'

back to her home she went the next day
crushed and broken upon her chair,
they had stolen her daughter away,
soon a hearing to decide what's fair.

how could they steal her child away?
one so innocent of fault was she,
in her arms her daughter should stay,
vibrant and laughing, a heart so free.

'Testimony of a woman is worth ½ that of a man..'

a trembling doe has lost her fawn
to specters imposing invented will,
her joy from heaven now seems gone,
the air in her home is now so still,

one hundred tears of the innocent flow,
prayers of the heart hidden within,
the comfort of angels to bestow,
to dry the sorrow from moistened skin.

'A man does not vow loyalty to a woman...'

winds ferocious started to spin..
not far away from the city near,
a huge wall of sand now to begin,
at dusk mowed forth it's monstrous sheer!

a mile away in a kangaroo court,
long bearded men gathered to deem,
one covered woman, her life to sort,
across the room, her daughter, her dream.

'A woman cannot be a judge or hold high public office...'

many beards spoke about the laws,
how she was unfit to be a mother,
defiance and evil were her flaws
and the child should be given to another.

the motion was made for a sentence to jail,
mayhaps a stoning for such a thing,
then all gasped as she removed her veil,
and stood like an angel about to take wing.

'A woman must have 4 male witnesses in order to prove rape...'

she looked to her daughter with the most brilliant of eyes
and began to sing in the tenderest of voice,
a sound with soft wings of bluebirds high,
the blessed choir of the heavens rejoice --

"Oh my daughter, you're heart is so pure,
sleep my sweet and kiss the sky,
with my love to hold you sure,
sleep my sweet and don't you cry"

'No woman is to publicly speak or sing in front of strangers...'

the quiet befell save a loudening growl,
windows swung open as did the door,
the room was caught in a deafening howl,
wind and sand tumbled in with a roar!

all sight and sound was taken away,
as souls all huddled on the ground,
for minutes like hours all would stay,
till quieted the sandstorm all around.

'Honor killing of women is legal...'

the long bearded mullahs stood upright
clearing their eyes from heaven's display,
the woman and child were nowhere in sight!
they must be found if they are to pay,

they searched the city upside and down,
everywhere one could possibly hide,
then said one bearded with a frown..
"to the desert they must have gone and died"

'Breaking of these laws may result in flogging or execution...'

years had passed, laws stayed strong,
but rumors from a city afar,
a woman and daughter to the place belonged,
started a school 'neath desert stars

they taught boys and girls science and math,
they taught of history, the world, everything,
but their favorite class they taught without wrath
was teaching the children to beautifully sing.